ISBN: 9781513615158

10 9 8 7 6 5 4 3 2                    0 8 1 7 1 6

Printed in the United States of America

♾This paper meets the requirements of ANSI/NISO Z39.48-1992 (Permanence of Paper)

# Table of Contents

# FOREWORD

## by Dr. Doris A. Derby

**The Color of Inspiration** gives women an innovative vehicle to pursue a pathway to self-discovery and fulfillment. It is a new kind of adult coloring book and reader which offers women pleasurable tools to personally reflect upon and creatively chart their own empowerment and rejuvenation. As one leafs through the inspiring drawings, informative texts, and thought provoking exercises, one travels spiritually through personal spaces with a suitcase of memories and dreams, and a purse filled with visions of new beginnings.

Nevaina Rhodes' book provides a creative technique for women to reveal and rejuvenate their core essence through its inspiration, meditation, self-dialogue written work, exercises and colorful expression. Initially one has the opportunity to make an "I Am" statement as the journey through the book is started. Each chapter's completion contributes to an image of who one is. One's vocabulary of self-perception is formed. It is a reflection of the thread which connects the seen and the unseen, the true self that expresses grace, joy, potential and circumstantial reality as it affirms one's purpose in life.

The act of coloring submerges one in experiences of childhood and adulthood simultaneously. It allows one to engage in deliberate gestures, experiential visualization, reconstruction of memories and the colorization of concrete images geared to the individual's own liking, priorities and personality. It is a form of therapy which provides a release for all of the baggage one often carries around and is weighted down by. Through coloring, personal and cultural identities, combined with shared experiences, conjure up visions of self-love, new expressions and new horizons.

**Dr. Doris A. Derby** is an educator, speaker, author, documentary photographer, visual and performing arts artist/producer and Civil Rights activist. Originally from New York City, she was the Founding Director of the Office of African American Student Services and Programs at Georgia State University in Atlanta from 1990 to 2012. While there she also served as Adjunct Associate Professor of Anthropology. She retired after 22 years of dedicated, creative and legendary service to continue her work in the arts, education, and the community. Her documentary photos have been shown locally, regionally and nationally in galleries, museums, books and documentary films. She is married to actor Bob Banks and they live in Atlanta, GA.

*About* Dr. Doris A. Derby

# Thank U's

**Thank God** from whom all blessings flow. Lord, this book was prayerfully written, and may the anointing destroy the yoke in all who reads it.

**Thank You to My Family,** Sam, Sallie, Gramel, Cuong, Bhisma, CeAvani, Couvade, and Chava...it takes a village to raise a book. Because you are...I CAN!

**Thank You to My Team "Manifest"** . . . artist, Keisha; graphics, Unique (eccentric design); printer, BookLogix. To my executive producer and mentor Dr. Doris Derby...you are spirit spoken...faith in action...money in motion! A writer is made better by the editor, thank you, Leslye Joy Allen for "perfectin' dem pages".

**Thank You** Jay White for showing me what innovative creative success looks like...I thrive in your shadow. Monique Merriweather Yarborough and Erika Campbell, thank you for sowing seed into good ground, may you reap a harvest of abundant returns. Even though "we ain't in college no mo' Toto! I am blessed to still be able to call you good friends who "believe." Kelvin Hoggard I pray you can see the fruit of your seed from heaven, I miss you my friend. Special thanks to the Westco Corp...it wouldn't be done without you! To my faithful friend and father in the faith, Pastor Derrick Rice of Sankofa United Church of Christ, thank you for covering me and this effort in prayer.

**All My Extended Family, Every Friend and Even Foe,** I thank you for strengthening my faith...the just shall live by it. Last, but certainly not least, thank you for getting this book. May you faithfully see it through to a desired end, discover yourself, and love who you find.

Welcome to a coloring journey to healing and wholeness that is truly unique. Whether you are 18 or 80-years-old, this book will help you release, imagine, and create. This Empowerment Guide is designed with you in mind.

*Get ready to Live! Laugh! Color!*

# Welcome . . .

Women are prone to address issues with a "fight or flight" response. Studies show that when there is a perceived threat of danger, the body readies itself for combat or escape. Many women of color are in this survival mode in their workplace, home life, and even their relationships.

This constant heightened state of adrenaline and physical tension is unhealthy and counterproductive, giving way to frustration, rage and other toxic emotions. For women of color, the labels such as the "angry black woman" rivaled only by the "strong black woman" often result. These tags imply that black women can endure infinite hardship without any recourse, relief or resolution, and keep on ticking.

Although this disposition is not true of all women of color, there is one distinct trait indigenous primarily to us...excess belly fat. Belly fat and other fatty deposits that give women of color their voluptuous curves, also release a hormone called epinephrine at a higher rate than other races. When this hormone is coupled with high stress levels, it becomes toxic in the body. In fact, stress is the common denominator in more than 90% of illness and diseases. Research has linked this "stress-factor" to women of color having a pre-disposition to certain illnesses.

This book is your practical place of refuge. Spending 15 to 30 minutes daily or weekly, reading, coloring, and working the pages of this book will empower, enlighten, and encourage you, while also developing a much needed routine of de-stressing.

Studies have shown that the methodical rhythm and sound of coloring can be relaxing. Color theory suggests that looking at certain colors can create particular moods in our minds, bodies and lives. Additionally, exploring the infinite depth of your potential will place you on a journey of self-discovery that will help to change you from the inside out. This book celebrates who you are and facilitates the discovery of who you can become.

Welcome to Your Journey!
Color On, Colored Girl.
The World is Waiting For You to Arrive.

*I am* who God says *I Am.*

# Identity

## Woman in White

Colorless without shade or hue…
a clean slate, a fresh start to "do you."
But who are you? Are you
the things that have happened in your past?
The stained choices, scolding voices, or relationships
that didn't last?
Are you your education, job or position…
are you a victim of your
circumstance or current condition.
You are a bright shiny ball of
unlimited possibility,
the unique idea of the Master of creativity.
You are what you think you are…
so master your thoughts and
create the identity you want.
Don't let the devil trick you with a fake ID.
Say to yourself…
I am who God says I am!

Draw, color, or doodle an inspired image here.

Create Your World

# I Am

Follow these easy steps:

1. Take three deep cleansing breaths . . . in through your nose, out through your mouth three times.

2. Close your eyes and imagine you are on the beach writing in the sand, smell the air, the sound of the waves and feel the sun on your face.

3. Write in the sand below as many feel good adjectives as you can think of that describe you as a person.

4. Color the picture and think about your many talents, gifts and abilities.

5. Meditate on the answer to this question: Who am I?

_____

_____

_____

_____

_____

_____

_____

_____

_____

_____

_____

*Write Your World*

# I Am Statement

For this exercise, I want you to describe who you are at your core. Not who you are in relationship to anyone else. For example, if I asked, "Who are you?" and you replied, "I am a wife," if you go through a divorce, you become an Ex-wife. Or, alternatively, you say, "I am the president of ABC Corporation." If your company downsizes, you become an Ex-president. I want you to think in terms that no one and nothing could ever put an "ex" in front of.

When Moses asked God, "Who shall I say sent me?" God replied, "I am that I am."

– Exodus 3:13-14

I pray the Spirit allows this

## I Am Statement

to reveal who God says you are.

Jesus asked Peter, "Who do you say that I am?" Christ pointed out that Peter's response could have only been revealed to him by the Holy Spirit.

– Matthew 16:15-16

A wonderful power coach by the name of Chloe Taylor Brown inspired this technique of creating what she calls a "mantra" which she says enables you to hold your position.

This easy-to-remember statement should reflect who you are presently, who you are becoming in the future…your hopes, potential and capacity… and how you want to use your gift to help others. It is our ability to serve others that gives our lives purpose and answers the question "Why was I created?"

This I AM statement anchors your identity and helps you deal with the rejection and disappointments that life can bring. By defining yourself, you are less likely to accept the definition that circumstances try to impose on you. You are not what has happened to you. You may need to leave this statement blank until you have completed more of the book, or you may have to make changes to it as you discover more things about yourself as you go through this workbook.

_____

_____

_____

_____

_____

_____

_____

_____

_____

_____

_____

_____

_____

_____

_____

*Write Your World*

# I Am Worksheet

Select 3 of the adjectives that BEST describe you from the sand, look up each in the dictionary and write the definition below.

Adjective: Definition

1. _____

2. _____

3. _____

Please find an example I AM statement below.

> Personal: I am power, love, and life. I can do anything, be anything, and have anything. I am created to succeed and help others to do the same. I am Nevaina.

This statement is a mantra for me that I say aloud regularly. As a professional actor, rejection is such a part of the territory that if I did not have a mechanism in place to help me keep things in perspective, my esteem could really take a beating. This has worked for me and I pray that it works for you.

I am _____, _____, _____.

I can_____.

I am created to_____.

Journal your thoughts, ideas, dreams, and feelings here.

_Write Your World_

# Meditation

## Woman in Brown

BROWN girl dancing in the moonlight

With her thick lips, full thighs, and hope in her eyes.

BROWN girl barely tinted, just slightly kissed by the sun

Is a sister through and through and know that she is one.

Caramel queen waiting at the bus stop

To take her into the city to her office on the top….

She is boss, baby all the way.

Dark mahogany woman

Skin rich like velvet drapes that cover and correct every mistake.

BROWN skin we can't see where you end

To the Earth, the roots run deep, follow the Nile and hear the ground speak

There she is…after so many years

I still recognize her.

She is coming back to me by finding herself.

Draw, color, or doodle an inspired image here.

*Create Your World*

Mediate.
Listen.
Know.

Journal your thoughts, ideas, dreams, and feelings here.

_Write Your World_

# Meditation

Meditation and prayer allow us to clear our minds so that we can identify what we want, recognize what it takes to achieve those things, remove obstacles from our path, and remain positive in the process.

Often times our to-do lists, and the demands of our life would suggest that we do not have time to meditate. Spending this quiet time is what will enable you to accomplish all of the things you must do on a daily basis. It will give you the grace that you need for the things that you cannot get done, and it will make you wise enough to know the difference.

Whatever is true, good, and pure and of good report focus on that. If there be any virtue in it, dwell on these things.
— Philippians 4:8

Creating a habit of rising early just to meditate for a few moments each day is priceless. Yet, for this next exercise, we are going to experience a guided meditation and journal the things that are revealed afterwards. This meditation tool can be used at any time and is beneficial to maintain balance throughout the day. Whether you are in the restroom or sitting in traffic and need to center yourself; perhaps you are able to create a more ideal setting by lighting a candle, listening to a nature sounds CD or a fountain. No matter the setting, whatever moments you can spend meditating will have valuable benefit.

# Meditation Worksheet

## STEP ONE:

## Clearing Your Mind

Start by bending your arms at the elbows and allowing your hands to come together about chest level. Your fingertips should be gently spread apart and one hand resting on the other.

If this is not a comfortable rest position then try your hands just relaxing and let your hands dangle by your side. Close your eyes and breathe 3 generous "cleansing breaths" (in through the nose, out through the mouth). Then relax into a normal breathing pattern, still inhale through your nose, and exhale through your mouth. With your eyes remaining closed, listen to the sound of your breathing. Try to focus on the sound of your own heartbeat. You may have to place your fingers over your ears or place one hand on your heart to do so.

The more you meditate, the easier and faster you will be able to hear your heart. As the sound of your breathing and heartbeat drown out everything else allow your mind to become blank.

If you are still not relaxed and mentally clear, try the 5 for 5 method…inhale for 5 counts, hold for 5 counts, exhale for 5, deny for 5 (deny means don't inhale again until a 5 count…it will make that next breath fuller by taking in more air). Repeat this cycle 3-5 times. Once a sense of stillness is achieved, continue to breathe and relax and move on to step 2.

# STEP TWO:

## *Guiding Your Thoughts*

Now that your mind is clear, random thoughts will still come into your head. I need you to have a "feel good" thought that you can use if anything adverse or contrary should come into your head. It could be the face of one of your children, a favorite vacation spot, or a picture that makes you smile. You should be able to think about that thing like a snap shot.

Again remember, the more that you meditate the easier it will be to draw positive energy automatically and the less you will have to use your "feel good" thought safe guard. Continue to breathe in and out with generous relaxing breaths. This breathing meditation may be all that you need to feel at ease and centered. For others you may want to move on to step 3.

# STEP THREE

## *Channel with Sound*

Allow a sound to come out of your mouth. It may be a sigh, a moan, it may even sound like baby talk or gibberish. Just a simple one or two syllable sound that can be repeated. It may change each time, or you may find a sound that really resonates with you and you want to stick with it.

Some Buddhists chant "Nam Myoho Renge Kyo," to prepare the mind for meditation. By releasing an organic sound you are able to subtly engage other senses in the experience, as well as channel your energy into meditation with more focus.

Maintain this posture and continue to keep your eyes closed as you continually repeat the steps. When you open your eyes, try to journal the things you felt, thought, and perceived while meditating.

Try saying this meditation prayer aloud either before or after you meditate:

May the words of my mouth and the meditation of my heart be acceptable in thy sight Oh Lord my strength and my redeemer.
                                                                — Psalm 19:14

_____
_____
_____
_____
_____
_____
_____
_____
_____
_____
_____
_____
_____
_____
_____
_____
_____
_____
_____

*Write Your World*

# Woman in Blue

BLUE got me with the blues,
slowly slipping into a Nina Simone mood.
Hot tea and a rainy day take me away
to the place of quiet thoughts
and peaceful moments
that are stolen, not bought.

Indigo hands dyed on the dusk…
daughters of the dusk that is.
Blue blooded, blue veins,
blues songs that changed thangs.
That screamed through the notes sultry and true
nothing like the blues to pull you through.
Go there and rest for a minute,
but don't stay—
return quickly to the sky blues
and good news of the day.
Tattered blue strings on ripped jeans
that fit her curves just right…
girl that must be them PZI's
that's brushing them thighs
and fitting your waist tight.
Blue sho' do look good on you!

Draw, color, or doodle an inspired image here.

*Create Your World*

*I will work while*
*I wait* **patiently.**

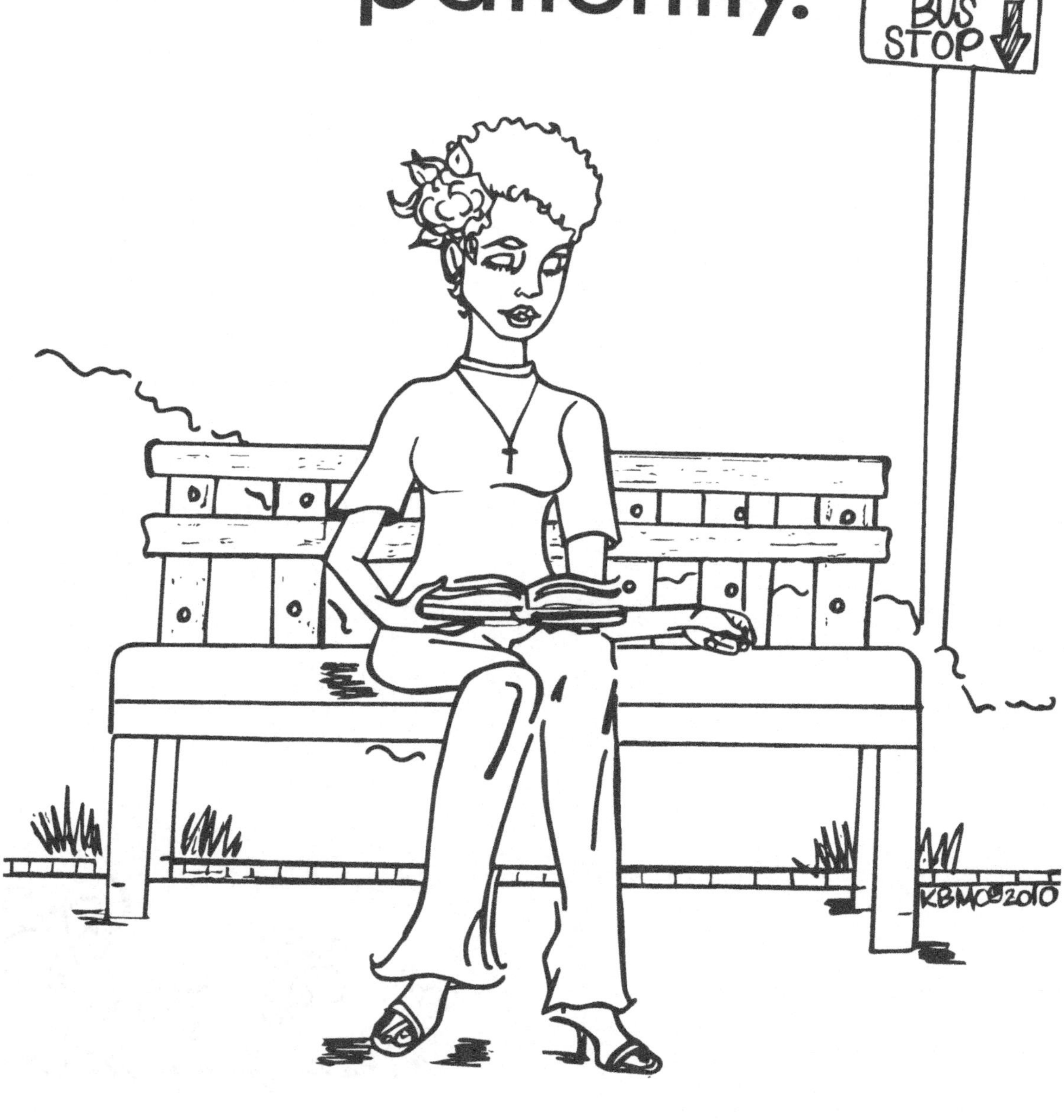

Journal your thoughts, ideas, dreams, and feelings here.

_____
_____
_____
_____
_____
_____
_____
_____
_____
_____
_____
_____
_____
_____
_____
_____
_____
_____
_____
_____
_____
_____
_____

*Write Your World*

# Patience

Patience is defined as the state of endurance under difficult circumstances, which can also mean persevering in the face of delay.

Let patience have her perfect work, that you may be perfect and entire, lacking nothing.

— James 1:4

Be still in the presence of the Lord, and wait patiently on Him to act.

— Psalm 37:7

I waited patiently for the Lord; and He inclined to me, and He heard my cry.

— Psalm 40:1

"*Patience is waiting*. Not passively waiting. That is laziness. But to keep going when the going is hard and slow-that is patience."

-Saint Augustine

It seems like when I go to the grocery store and I am in a rush, I always get behind the person who has a million coupons for things they did not buy, or there is no bar-code on half of the things in their cart, or even I have managed to pick up the one item that does not have a tag, and the end result is I have to wait. I sometimes take these moments as signs that life is giving me another chance to learn to wait. The reality is if I want to buy the items, I have no choice but to wait.

Consider this, wouldn't it be better for God to show up and you can say… "I knew You were coming all the time." Than for Him to manifest and find you waiting as though you had no faith He was going to come.

I remember when I was a little girl, my granddaddy would tell me that he was going to take me somewhere and I would sit on the couch looking out the window for him to come. He would hardly ever show up at the exact time he said he was going to be there, but he would always come.

I stayed ready for when he would arrive, many times it would be just to take a simple trip to get ice cream. He would always get whatever I ordered…a pineapple sundae made with chocolate ice cream, wet walnuts and whipped cream. I know my granddaddy loved me …as an adult, I cannot even eat half of one of those sundaes, it's so sweet… but he would eat the whole thing.

We should wait on God in a way that says, "I knew you were going to come through for me." This displays patience with a purpose.

_____

_____

_____

_____

_____

_____

_____

_____

_____

*Write Your World*

# Patience Worksheet

List five things that you are waiting for God to do in your life. For example: healing from a disease, mending a broken relationship, losing weight, getting a good night sleep. Nothing is too small or too large, but let it be things that you have put into works or been waiting to manifest.

1. _____

2. _____

3. _____

4. _____

5. _____

List one scripture that applies to each item on your list. You can use the biblical concordance, or use Google online with a word search. Read these scriptures aloud when you get doubtful or when it seems as though your faith is running low.

1. _____

2. _____

3. _____

4. _____

5. _____

For each of these things imagine what the ideal resolution would be. For example you might visualize the doctors telling you that the cancer is completely gone ...see yourself sitting in the doctor's office receiving that news. Imagine it in as much detail as possible—your clothes, the room, etc. Repeat this process with each item.

Journal your thoughts, ideas, dreams, and feelings here.

_Write Your World_

# Woman in Orange

Orange tiger lilies dance in the wind just for you.

Autumn leaves rustle from the trees just for you.

Even that orange line across the horizon

when the sun sets is just for you….

lest you forget how spectacular and special you are.

I made you….

Just for me, said the Creator in a

Whisper that floated on orange dust and

Settled in your heart….

Renewing your hope and

Restoring your soul…

Draw, color, or doodle an inspired image here.

Create Your World

My *Hope* is the Seed of My *Faith*; it **Grows** and **Grows.**

Journal your thoughts, ideas, dreams, and feelings here.

_Write Your World_

# Hope

Hope as defined by Webster's is to expect with confidence or to desire with expectation of obtainment.

For we are saved by hope; but hope that is seen is not hope. For if you see it, why do you hope for it.

– Romans 8:24

President Obama's retort during his campaign is one of my favorite quotes, he said, "But in the unlikely story that is America, there has never been anything false about hope." I have heard so many older black people say that they never thought they would see the day when a black man would be president, but now their hopes have been realized, not once, but twice over. Many speculate about the efficacy and success of his presidency, but it is an undeniable reality. Hope is what this nation needed then, and needs even more now.

"The very least you can do in your life is to figure out what you *hope* for. And the most you can do is live inside that *hope*. Not admire it from a distance but live right in it, under its roof."

-Novelist Barbara Kingsolver

OTHER HOPE QUOTES:

"We must accept finite **disappointment**, but we must never lose *infinite hope*."

-Dr. Martin Luther King Jr.

"*Hope* is the companion of power and the mother of success; for who so hopes strongly has within him the gift of *miracles*."

-Samuel Smiles

"Consult not your **fears** but your *hopes* and *dreams*. Think not about your **frustrations**, but about your *unfulfilled potential*."

-Pope John XXIII

# Hope Worksheet

List five things that you hope to accomplish in the next 30 days.

1. _____
2. _____
3. _____
4. _____
5. _____

List 5 things that you hope to accomplish in the next 6 months.

1. _____
2. _____
3. _____
4. _____
5. _____

List 5 things that you hope to accomplish within the next year.

1. _____
2. _____
3. _____
4. _____
5. _____

Journal your thoughts, ideas, dreams, and feelings here.

*Write Your World*

# WOMAN IN RED

RED like bloodshed from busted lips,

like garter belts on wide hips,

swinging to the tune of a upbeat number,

red like the passion of a tender lover.

It was the lipstick stain

that changed everything,

the color I saw

when she said his name.

It is the color I wear

when I don't care…I will not be ignored.

I dance in it, prance in it,

and steal every glance in it.

You cannot be quiet, numb, or dead

when wearing red.

It was the blood that was shed just for me

so that I could be emotionally free.

It is the colorstone…

the color of the cornerstone…of my faith.

Draw, color, or doodle an inspired image here.

*Create Your World*

# I Am *Creating* the *Gift* of My Tomorrow, *Today.*

Journal your thoughts, ideas, dreams, and feelings here.

_Write Your World_

# faith

The dictionary says that faith is a loyalty to something, a conviction about something for which there is no proof, trust or belief in God, or the practice of religious conviction.

For I say through the grace given unto me, to every man not to think more highly of himself than he ought for to each man God has given a measure of faith.

- Romans 12:3

Without faith it is impossible to please God.

- Hebrews 11:6

Faith without work is dead.

- James 2:20

Let's take a look at the tangible things that are associated with the intangible element called "faith".

Now faith is the substance of things hoped for and the evidence of things not seen.

- Hebrews 11:1

# SUBSTANCE:

Essential nature; ultimate reality that underlies all outward manifestations and change.

# EVIDENCE:

An outward sign, something that furnishes proof.

# WORKS:

An activity in which one exerts strength or faculties to perform a specific task or duty that is often part or a phase of a larger activity.

## These definitions tend to dismantle the colloquialism "blind faith."

Faith is very focused and deliberate. If we have faith that we can build a house on an empty lot, we go through certain steps to make that happen.

We get an architect and a general contractor who know something about building a house—they bring the substance—the essence, the skills, the knowledge. They may create blue prints or a small scale model—that is the evidence—tangible signs of certain manifestation.

Lastly, the crew starts to build the house one brick, one wall, and one window at a time...that is the works—the effort and the energy exerted in a deliberate direction towards a desired end. Soon, what was once an empty lot, is now a house.

# Faith Worksheet

Look at your hope list and write down five things that are part of the substance that is needed to achieve each item. It may be resources, materials, knowledge or relationships that are related to the specific thing.

1. _____
2. _____
3. _____
4. _____
5. _____

Write down a timeline and end result for each item on your substance list. For example if one of the things you hope for is to have your own interior design firm, you may start with a company name and business plan to be completed in one month. Repeat this step for each item on the list above.

1. _____
2. _____
3. _____
4. _____
5. _____

Write down 5 specific works that you can do to reach each goal within the timeline. Using the same example, in order to get the business plan completed in a month, one item might be to spend two hours daily writing out the particulars of the business. Note: for this example, you might need to add learning how to develop a business plan to your substance list.

1. _____

2. _____

3. _____

4. _____

5. _____

If you don't know where to start, start where you are! Only you know your current knowledge base and the things that you need to do in order to move to the next step. A good way to find out the recipe of a good sweet potato pie is to ask someone who has baked them successfully many times before. Look around you, your support system is probably in place. And nowadays, the internet is an exceptional resource for finding out what you do not know.

The biblical prophet, Elijah, told the widow woman to go to her neighbors and borrow vessels, then put the oil that she had in her house in those vessels in order to pay her taxes, keep her son, and sustain her household. He basically, told her to look around and ask for the help that she needed to add to what she already had in her possession. (Reference II Kings 4:1-7)

God has a way of putting resources in our lives once we make the choice to do the work to change our situation. It is my prayer that on this worksheet, you will write the game plan, make it plain, and God will send you provision for the vision as you diligently walk out step-by-step this faith plan.

# Joy

# Woman in Yellow

YELLOW is the color of the

hidden Rockefeller line,

you seen 'dem signs…

will buy your gold!

All the yellow rocks being bought and sold.

But your soul is golden,

not for sale, and don't let it be stolen.

Polish it daily, and feed it sunshine

so that you smile from the inside.

Stay inside the yellow lines,

don't stray to the left or to the right,

but keep your inner light.

I SEE YOU …

shine on, sunshine, shine

Draw, color, or doodle an inspired image here.

*Create Your World*

My Mood, Choice.

Journal your thoughts, ideas, dreams, and feelings here.

_____

_____

_____

_____

_____

_____

_____

_____

_____

_____

_____

_____

_____

_____

_____

_____

_____

_____

_____

_____

_____

_____

_____

*Write Your World*

# Joy

Joy is one of the fruits of the spirit identified in Galatians and is essential to maintaining a healthy, happy life. Some definitions suggest that joy is the actual capacity to enjoy life. Let us examine this concept called joy which I submit is an inner peace, and optimistic disposition that is not contingent upon what is happening around you.

This is the day that the Lord has made, I shall rejoice and be glad in it.

– Psalm 118:24

A cheerful heart is good medicine, but a crushed spirit dries up the bones.

– Proverbs 17:22

You will go out in joy and be led forth in peace; the mountains and hills will burst into song before you, and all the trees of the field will claps their hands.

– Isaiah 55:1

The psalmist said "This joy that I have, the world didn't give it to me." God is the only one who can give the gift of true joy. The Word is the inner witness that compels our Spirit to rejoice even if our flesh is weak. The rejoicing of our inner spirit creates an outer expression of joy.

What is the joy of the Lord? Christ found His joy in keeping the commandments of God.

John 15:10-11 If you keep My commandments, you will abide in My love, just as I have kept my Father's commandments and abide in His love. These things have I spoken to you, that My joy may remain in you, and that your joy may be full.

There is a grave pitfall in allowing our joy to fade. When you look at Genesis 4:6-7, God asked Cain, "Why are you so angry? And why has your countenance fallen? If you do well, are you not accepted? And if you do not, sin lies at the door. And its desire is for you, but you should rule over it."

We must be mindful to handle disappointment and frustrated intentions with a spirit of joy. It is this joyful disposition that allows us to recover. When your joy leaves, your hope, faith, and belief take a beating. It is hard to move forward because your energy is drained. A lack of joy can cause you to sabotage opportunities and abort purpose.

_____

_____

_____

_____

_____

_____

_____

_____

_____

_____

_____

_____

_____

_____

_____

_____

_____

_____

_____

_____

*Write Your World*

# Joy Worksheet

Anita Baker put it well when she sang, "You bring me joy, when I'm down. Oh so much joy, when I lose my way, I can remember your smile…You bring me joy."

In this exercise, I want you to create your joy list. List ten things that bring you joy. It may be a favorite black dress, or the memory of having your first child. Whatever brings you joy, write it down. Remembering the things on this list will help to bring your countenance up in times when it seems low.

1. _____

2. _____

3. _____

4. _____

5. _____

6. _____

7. _____

8. _____

9. _____

10. _____

FOR A QUICK JOY FIX TRY THE FOLLOWING:

- Laugh out loud for no reason.
- Clap your hands and give yourself a round of applause like you are your own biggest fan.
- Jump up and down (work the "jump for joy" premise.)
- Dance while singing your favorite song. (Motown hits are great for this one!)
- Make funny faces at yourself in the mirror.
- Tickle your own feet.
- Throw a tantrum like a three year old…the stomping, screaming, lying on the floor kicking kind.
- Make fart noises with your arm pit.

These things may sound silly, but God uses the foolish things to confound the wise. It may be just the glimpse of levity you need to shift your perspective to the positive. Maybe you can laugh just long enough to remember that weeping may endure for the night, but JOY comes in the morning!

_____

_____

_____

_____

_____

_____

_____

_____

_____

*Write Your World*

# Woman in Purple

PURPLE rain falling on royalty.
She moves with her neck
outstretched in expectation,
eating grapes and growing wise,
amethyst and opal line her eyes.
Nobility personified,
robes, and gemstones dignified.
Purple hazed intoxicated
with the clearest of mind
for we are not high on drugs or wine
but spiritually elevated
...and the view is
wonderful from up here.

Draw, color, or doodle an inspired image here.

I Notice What *I See*; I Focus on *My Vision*.

Journal your thoughts, ideas, dreams, and feelings here.

_Write Your World_

# Vision

My people perish from a lack of knowledge.

– Hosea 4:6

Where there is no vision the people perish.

– Proverbs 29:18

Write the vision, make it plain on tablets, so that he who reads it may run with it.

– Habakkuk 2:2

Many self-help instructors and motivational speakers agree that a vision statement can be one of the initial keys to success. Fortune 500 companies use them in the form of a mission statement. Some companies have both. Their vision statements represent who they are and what they represent as a company and the mission statement outlines what they want to do with who they are... answering the question "Why do we exist?"

A vision statement is a road map for you to follow that will keep you motivated and on course. You might start with your desired destination, then the course that you will take to get there, and why you are going to that destination. In essence, a vision statement tells who, when, why, and how. It guides the reader to a specific desired end.

A vision statement example: RAW Empowerment will generate a million dollars in sales within two years by offering inspirational goods and services to people nationwide to help them live better lives.

If you are not sure of your mission or purpose, you may refer to your hope list for inspiration. Using the knowledge of what you enjoy or are called to do, will help you to create your vision statement. This is different from your I AM statement, which was more of a personal vision statement. This vision statement speaks to your purpose: that which you create, offer, and deliver to the world through your profession or passionate pursuits.

_____

_____

_____

_____

_____

_____

_____

_____

_____

_____

_____

_____

_____

_____

_____

_____

_____

_____

_____

_____

*Write Your World*

# Vision Worksheet

A 3 Step Process to Create a Vision Statement:

## PROFESSIONAL: VISUALIZE, IDENTIFY, ACTUALIZE

## PERSONAL: INTENTION, MOTIVATION, ACTION

1. VISUALIZE: Take a few moments to dream about what you would do if you had no boundaries. What would you try if you knew that you could not fail? Imagine yourself in the ideal position and place, surrounded by all of the right people. If you could start your own business what would it be. Imagine yourself working in that business, hiring employees, expanding to a franchise, receiving awards and accolades for your success. This is the WHAT of your vision statement. This approach can also be applied to your personal endeavors. In the personal realm, this element is called INTENTION. What is it that you want to do? It might be to meet someone new, travel somewhere you have never been, lose 35 lbs. Whatever the case, identify a particular intention.

2. IDENTIFY: the mission, purpose or function of your business, effort, company, or idea? What is the scope of your effort… local, national, international, global? What is the target market of your goods or service? Imagine that you are being interviewed by a newspaper and they are asking you questions about the history of your company, the secrets to your success, and what makes you different from anyone else, why are you unique? This is the WHY of your vision statement.

On the personal front, we refer to this as MOTIVATION. This is why you want to do a certain thing. For example: Meeting someone new...because you would like to be married, you want to expand your social circle, you want to socialize more.

3.  ACTUALIZE: now articulate step one and two in a concise statement, adding the WHEN and the HOW. "When," establishes the timeline for your success. "HOW" is a summary of the mission statement, which outlines the specific goods and services that you will offer, the quality of your efforts, and the benefits realized by those who partake of your goods and services.

    Personally, we call this step ACTION. How will you go about accomplishing the intentions that you have identified...what specifically will you do? Using our base example: Meeting someone new. You might try going to a singles social and make a conscious effort to talk to at least 10 new people while there, or you may go to the bookstore and introduce yourself to 2 new people each time you go. Perhaps you are open to trying an Internet social site. Be as specific as possible about the actions you will take. When our intentions, motivations and actions are all in alignment, the chances of us being successful in our endeavor are greatly increased.

When we actually write down our vision, we are more likely to commit our thoughts and actions toward it. Plan your work and work your plan; that is how writing your vision statement for your professional and personal lives can benefit you.

VISION STATEMENT:

_____

_____

_____

_____

Create a Vision Board:

Get out your magazines and cut out pictures of images that you desire to see, have, and accomplish in your life. Invite your girlfriends over; spread out on your living room floor and have a Vision Board party! Be sure to place your finished board where you can see it at the start and end of your day. You will be surprised how effective Vision Boards can be and how the power of attraction will bring the things you visualize into your life.

Commit your works to the Lord and your thoughts will be established.

– Proverbs 16:3

_Write Your World_

# Mid-Way Motivation

by DeVetta Holman Nash, MPH, NCAS-III
Associate Director, Counseling and Wellness
University of North Carolina-Chapel Hill

## Relax, Release and Relate . . .

Anxiety and Fear are the #1 causes of Stress for any individual. When these factors are omnipresent and live within a human vessel on a daily, consistent basis, it is a formula for mental, emotional and physical ruin. Stress has become the umbrella term for many causes of mental, emotional and even some physical issues. When we look at the stress experienced by a majority of African American women, it is usually caused by external factors….those things we absolutely have no control over like racism, work place harassment, discrimination, cultural alienation…….and just life in general. But, whatever the reason or the causes of stress, usually, it is one's REACTION to the situation that informs and determines how it affects the body overall.

In an era where the "strong black woman" is synonymous with strength, resiliency, multitasking, bringing home the bacon and cooking it too……many women of African American descent will "keep on keeping on," even when warning signs are glaring and lights are flashing and signaling us to stop and "sit down"! As a people, we endure against the odds and proudly proclaim Maya Angelou's, "And Still I Rise." How do I know this? I know this because I am one of those women. Black women, in general, know about persevering and persisting. However, as strong Black women we may not know that we lag behind Whites and other women in national health and mental health indices. The depression rate in African American women is reported to be almost 50% higher than that of Caucasian women. Blacks, and Black women in particular, account for approximately 25% of the mental and emotional health needs in the United States; yet, we make up only 12 per cent of the national population. When you couple this fact with the attitudinal dynamics of being ambivalent and reticent about seeking mental health care, therein lies a brewing formula for disaster.

We might ask ourselves this question: "What is the value of being strong, if we melt down and deteriorate in the process? Our obituaries will read magnificently, but the battle would have been fought for naught. Implicit in all of this is the fact that stress has a high correlation to coronary heart disease, which is the #1 killer of African American women. Stress can cause metabolic acidosis, which is a condition that occurs when the body produces too much acid or when the kidneys are not removing enough acid from the body. Causes are diverse, but this condition is reportedly linked to stress. Needless to say, stress is a major contributor of high blood pressure.

Let these and other conditions be a reality check in our lives. It is now or never to decide what no other person can decide for us. Reclaiming our lives, controlling our thoughts, being mindful about what we allow to infiltrate our spirits is within our reach. For a minute, peacefully think about what you can do to decrease, reduce and hopefully, diminish the stress(ors) in your life:

a. **Prioritize**…do that which is necessary and let the rest wait on you

b. **Remember**…there is only one of you and the human vessel is yours to nurture and value

c. **Awaken**…your mind to massages, meditation, yoga, aromatherapy, and bio-feedback…some stress-reducing fragrance oils to use during your massage or aromatherapy are jasmine, ylang ylang, patchouli, lavender, sandalwood and sage

d. **Imagine**…yourself being someplace that you truly love and remain there for at least 20-30 minutes each day

e. **Stay**…spiritually focused and arm yourself with powerful, prophetic, scriptural words of inspiration

f. **Exercise**…keep it moving!! Walk at least 20 minutes each day to improve your cardiovascular health, as well as, your mental and emotional health

g. **Surround**…yourself with positive, forward thinking people and a strong social support system.

It never fails, when **PRAISES** go up, **BLESSINGS** come down.

Yes, Sisters….we are too blessed to be stressed!

Journal your thoughts, ideas, dreams, and feelings here.

_Write Your World_

# Woman in Green

GREEN like grass stained white trousers on a summer day,

like cash packed pockets on payday,

like the trees that stretch to reach the sky,

each limb sending praises to the most high.

Like palm trees planted roots deep,

deep beneath the Earth.

Unable to be moved

when things go from bad to worse.

It is the plant that pushes through the dirt

to greet the marvelous light,

like the grass covered motherlands too rich,

to be blown dry by the harsh winds of life.

A life giving, breathtaking fortress,

a marvel to examine.

A mountain lined valley that is lush

EVEN in the time of famine.

Draw, color, or doodle an inspired image here.

*Create Your World*

Money Comes *Easily, Frequently,* and *Abundantly.*

I Am a Money Magnet.

I Pay for *What I Need* and Save for *What I Want.*

I Am a Money Magnet.

Journal your thoughts, ideas, dreams, and feelings here.

_Write Your World_

# Financial Wealth

Above all things, I pray you prosper and be in good health, even as your soul prospers.

- 3 John 1:2

Using this as the anchor scripture, let's look at financial, physical, and soul (mind, will and emotions) wealth.

MONEY SCRIPTURES:

A feast is made for laughter, and wine maketh merry; but money answers all things..

- Ecc. 10:19

One man pretends to be rich, yet has nothing; another pretends to be poor, yet has great wealth.

- Proverbs 13:7

In the house of the wise are the stores of choice food and oil, but a foolish man devours all he has.

- Proverbs 21:20

There is a difference between money and wealth. Money is a tender or a measure for the rate of exchange. Wealth in one definition is the accumulation of large sums of money. In another definition, offered by financial guru, Robert Kiyosaki—Money is the ability to survive days forward. For example a storehouse of clean drinking water when Katrina hit made a person more wealthy than a mattress full of dollar bills.

Women are far more susceptible to spending money on consumer goods, be it clothes, shoes, make-up, hair, household items, etc. Yet, we are not as likely to invest money in things that will bring a financial return or help to secure our futures and those of our loved ones. The picture you colored illustrates that we can attract money to us with our thinking, but what will you do with the abundance of money that is coming your way? Good stewardship over our blessings is crucial to insure that our blessings do not bring sorrow with it.

When a person is wealth-minded and not money-minded, they are less like to fall into the pitfalls of sin and indulgent materialism. We have to change the way we think about money and examine our feelings toward money and those who have it. What is money for? How do we earn it? How do we use it? When we use our small bit of resources…a little money here and there…to accumulate wealth or a significant piece of money, then we can invest and create streams of income that produce residual returns. This is when you have reached the level of being able to afford luxury items.

Today's culture of consumerism has the Smiths trying to keep up with the Joneses, and the Joneses are in debt up to their eyeballs. Neither the Smiths nor the Joneses can afford it, but they are trying to keep up with celebrities and commercialized trends in an effort to maintain a luxury-filled lifestyle.

Take a break from buying all that you see on television and mass media marketing…instagram snapshots will have people flocking to hot spots and pawn shops to keep up their "insta-images." Consider focusing on building wealth, establishing an inheritance, and fortifying your financial future.

# Financial Wealth Worksheet

In order to be wealthy, you have to be financially healthy and this is a part of your financial physical. Keep a financial diary for a week. Keep all of your receipts—a manila envelope works well. At the end of the week, take all of the receipts and tally up your spending. Fill in the totals as they apply.

## TOTALS SPENT ON NEEDS TO SURVIVE.

Items associated with these basic needs for survival.

Drinkable water, food, shelter, clothing and ability to keep clean.

Food/water $_____spent

Shelter and vital utilities $_____spent

Clothing/ Laundry $_____spent

We will factor into the shelter equation the ability to keep clean necessity as water bill costs. Cell phones, home phones, cable, internet and other non-survival related costs must go into the luxury category as they are not essential for life although many of us may feel like we would die without them.

# TOTAL SPENT ON LUXURY OR OPTIONAL ITEMS.

Food bought eating out $ _____spent

(Although take-out has become essential in our lives, it is not necessary and the tremendous cost can be avoided by cooking at home.)

Designer clothing $ _____spent

(same as above; not anymore capable of clothing you than regular or less expensive garments)

Shoes, handbags, and accessories $ _____spent

Car payment $ _____spent

(You may say you NEED your car, but you will not die without it. This is a luxury not survival item)

Cost associated with vehicle (gas, maintenance, etc.) $ _____spent

Cell phone/home phone $ _____spent

Internet, cable, movie rentals $ _____spent

Entertainment expenses $ _____spent

All other expenses not mentioned $ _____spent

$ _____spent

$ _____spent

Kiyosaki, author of *Rich Dad, Poor Dad*, suggests that your luxury purchases should be made from your investments. If you have no investment or residual income then you are not in a position to make luxury purchases. It is debatable, as to how strictly this ideal should be followed, but I will ask this question, "Is your current financial state working for you?" Is the percentage of money that is going to optional items a reflection of what you think your priorities are or should be? How important is your ability to survive and your ability to help insure the survival of your loved ones? Is that reflected in the totals?

One suggestion to combat the inclination to spend more than you earn and buy things that you do not need is to increase your relationship with God. This will help to reduce your desire to fill voids with material things. The second suggestion is to increase your savings and put a portion of your savings into things that help you to survive.

You are already wealthier than over 90% of the world's population if you have access to toilets and clean running water. You have to think like a wealthy person and start to invest. Wise investments are those things that will make money for you. Only borrow money to make money, not just to spend it. Borrow to EARN not to BURN.

_____

_____

_____

_____

_____

_____

_____

_____

_____

_____

_____

_____

_____

_____

_____

_____

_____

_____

_____

_____

*Write Your World*

Draw, color, or doodle an inspired image here.

*Create Your World*

# Physical Wealth

Being physically able to enjoy the new "you" that you are creating is—"priceless." Women of Color have a higher predisposition to many diseases and illness. African-American women are particularly more likely to suffer from diseases, disability and early death at a higher rate than any other minority group. Factors such as medical system distrust, delayed or inadequate treatment and diagnosis, poverty, racism and genetics all play a part in this statistic. We must also look at lifestyle choices, weight, and cultural habits that are not conducive to good health.

You can even look at the way that we cook and eat. Many other cultures have healthier dining habits than do African-American women. Fried, fast and calorie rich foods all lend to our demise at an accelerated rate. Obesity among African-American women is categorically worse than any other group. Sixty-six percent of black women are overweight and 37 percent of those are technically obese, meaning that they are more than 30 percent over their ideal body weight. Mexican women trail closely behind with 66 percent being overweight and 33 percent being obese. Across the board, all races of women; including Caucasians, are statistically more overweight than in decades prior.

We have to take charge of our physical well-being. We must develop eating habits that include more fruits, vegetables, and water. Many free clinics offer nutritionists who will work with you to develop a diet that is suited for your blood and body type. Again the internet is an excellent source of health information to provide preventative and alternative natural methods to weight loss and healthy living. This is not an endorsement for the billion dollar weight loss industry which seduces people to buy plans, pills, and programs that may or may not work. This is a plea for you to reach a healthy weight and help your body work for you and not against you.

Exercise is an important part of this regiment. Walking for a few minutes a day can make a tremendous difference in your energy level, weight, and level of focus. If not that, put on your favorite Mary J Blige CD, turn it to a fast tune and dance around the house. Move, stretch, dance…Do something! I recently started doing more work in the yard and around the house and it is amazing the difference that it makes.

We must also be vigilant about our sexual health. Too many of us are being ravaged by AIDS and other preventable diseases because we are putting ourselves at risk in our sexual relationships, and neglecting our responsibility to take care of our temples. We desire to be loved, touched, appreciated, but it should not be at the risk of our lives. Use protection! Get tested! Be wise. It only takes one time to have sex to get HIV…just one! And for those of you who may be living with HIV or AIDS, a healthy lifestyle and early proactive interventions are critical for you to live a long and happy life.

Don't allow fear to cripple you when it comes to hereditary diseases. You can be the first in your family to break the cycle by deliberately making different choices. It is important to differentiate when you are dealing with a hereditary illness versus an illness that is a product of lifestyle. As we said before, God is able to deliver us out of them all, but you must know the works that need to accompany your faith for your healing. In the physical wealth worksheet, we will look at some scriptures that you can use to encourage yourself.

We still believe in God being a God of miracles. I have a girlfriend who was diagnosed as HIV positive after taking a saliva test. We began to pray and fast for her deliverance to be confirmed. When she had the follow-up blood tests, they all came back negative. Her faith, made her whole. I believe that the miracles of God are not bound by the source, nature or severity of the illness. He said he came to heal all manner of sickness, illness, and disease, albeit cancer, heart disease, or AIDS…God can heal you. Until that healing is manifest, work your faith.

Put your energy towards the desired end of being healthy by any and all means available to you. Take your healing by force by making choices to lead to wellness.

We only get one life and one body in which to live it…embrace it for the miraculous craftsmanship that it is. You have heard the saying, "God don't make junk." It is very important that we don't treat our bodies like junk. Make the commitment to yourself today to live a better and healthier life.

I Am Fearfully and Wonderfully Made.

*I Am Enough.*

Journal your thoughts, ideas, dreams, and feelings here.

_Write Your World_

# Physical Wealth Worksheet

Start by saying this affirmation aloud:

# I am committed to being

# *healthy, wealthy, and wise.*

Current weight: _____    Ideal weight: _____

(Ideal weight can be based on medical speculations, or your own personal comfort weight. Just set a real goal in pounds.)

Current amount of time spent weekly doing physical activity: _____

Goal amount of time spent weekly doing physical activity: _____

List five physical activities that you can do to reach your goal.

1. _____
2. _____
3. _____
4. _____
5. _____

Suggestions include: walking, yard work, club dancing, house dancing, belly dancing, yoga, stretching, light weightlifting, kickboxing, skating, rigorous housework, cheerleading practice (volunteer and follow along), part-time job at FED EX, ( if you can lift minimal weight you can get a work out and earn extra cash). Brainstorm some other ideas and ask some of your girlfriends what they do to stay in shape.

Keep a food journal for a full day by writing down everything you eat.

# Breakfast:

_____
_____
_____
_____

# Lunch:

_____
_____
_____
_____

# Dinner:

_____

_____

_____

_____

# Between Meal Snacks:

_____

_____

_____

_____

What is the approximate percentage of food consumed from each group:

Fruits and Vegetables: _____

Meats and proteins: _____

Grains and carbohydrates: _____

Milk and Dairy: _____

Sweets and Snacks: _____

How many glasses of water have you had today? Are you anywhere near your 8 glasses?

Number of glasses of water: _____ Ideal number of glasses of water: 8 glasses

Draw, color, or doodle an inspired image here.

*Create Your World*

# Soul Wealth

The soul is comprised of the mind, will and emotions…let's look at each individually.

*For God has not given us the spirit of fear, but of power, love, and a sound mind.*

*– 2 Timothy 1:7*

## The Mind:

A sound mind is a gift of the Spirit—an inalienable right of the believer. Two possible things that effect the mind are our thoughts and the use of mind-altering drugs.

If you fill your mind with negative thoughts then it will cause your mind to become pessimistic, depressed, and gloomy. However, if you fill your mind with positive thoughts then the mind is encouraged to create, thrive and be vibrant.

The mind is intangible…we can see and study the brain, but the mind remains illusive, and complex. It is the Spirit of a person that animates the mind, the mind that animates the body, and the body that animates the life of a person—All interconnected and collaborating to accomplish the goal of living.

Many people use mind-altering drugs to escape life… to numb the pain and dull the senses to the confusion. But I submit that whatever you are trying to forget, avoid, or deny by using drugs will still be there once you are sober minded again. Therefore we are going to create a thought pattern to free you from addiction and the use of habitual drugs.

I know people who have been miraculously delivered from deep addictions by first admitting that they had a problem. They openly acknowledged that the drug use was not good for them or their loved ones. They prayed in faith that God would remove the desire for cigarettes, alcohol, crack and other addictive drugs from them. I know others who made the choice to go into rehabilitation programs to be liberated, but it started with the acknowledgment that there was a problem.

The willing and the obedient shall eat of the fat of the land.

– Isaiah 1:19

Not my will, but thy will be done.

– Luke 22:42

**The Will:** These scriptures imply that man does have a will of his own and must make the conscious choice to surrender that will to God. Free will has been perceived as a license to do what you want to do. We even have a song about it… "it's your thang, do what you want to do."

However, in the life of the believer, we should desire the will of God for our lives, not out of obligation or fear of the "God's gonna get you theory," which creates a feeling of bondage. Yet, out of our love for God and our understanding that His ways are higher than our own and designed for our benefit…this approach brings a spirit of liberation.

We must also release ourselves from condemnation when we miss the mark. When we mess up, God forgives and throws it into the sea of forgetfulness.

You have to give yourself permission to forgive yourself and move forward pass your mistake. It is God's will that you make it to the mark of the high calling, not that you are permanently derailed when you stumble.

Lastly, **The Emotions:** This is particularly significant in the lives of women, as we tend to naturally be more emotional. If you throw PMS or pregnancy hormones in the mix, we can be an emotional mess. The Bible says in Proverbs 16:32 "Whosoever is slow to anger is better than the mighty; and he who rules his spirit than he who takes the city." (The lower case "s" in spirit indicates that this is our emotional self and not the indwelling Spirit of God).

We are meant to control our emotions, not allow our emotions to control us. Control does not mean to be emotionless, but it means that your emotions should propel the passion, tenacity, and stamina you need to do the things you desire and accomplish the goals you identify. It should move you forward, NOT hold you back or get you off track.

_Write Your World_

# Soul Worksheet

For those who live according to the flesh, set their minds on the things of the flesh, but those who live according to the Spirit, set their minds on things of the spirit.

— Romans 8:39

# Do you have

# stinkin' thinkin'?

Everything begins as a thought…thoughts are things. Thoughts produce actions and actions produce manifestations. Set your timer for 5 minutes and I want you to write down everything you think about in that five minutes…from the most mundane thought of "Do I want grape jelly or strawberry on my PBJ" to the most profound "I am going to file for divorce today." Afterwards examine the thoughts that have spiritual significance in your life and which are the thoughts that distract you from growing.

Draw, color, or doodle an inspired image here.

*Create Your World*

# *Thought List*

1. _____
2. _____
3. _____
4. _____
5. _____
6. _____
7. _____
8. _____
9. _____
10. _____
11. _____
12. _____
13. _____
14. _____
15. _____
16. _____
17. _____

# Will & Actions

Write down 3 things that you strongly believe you should or should not do. For example: I strongly believe that people should not live together before they get married. Or I strongly believe that spanking a child is needed.

1. I strongly believe that _____
   _____
   _____
   _____

2. I strongly believe that _____
   _____
   _____
   _____

3. I strongly believe that _____
   _____
   _____
   _____

Now you will have to do some Bible research to find 2 or 3 scriptures that support your belief, or you may find 2 or 3 scriptures that dispel your belief. Remain open, if you are ready to say "not my will but thy will be done."

You may also want to seek Godly counsel for conversations about anything that you are conflicted or unsure about. The mind will justify whatever the heart desires and the heart can deceive us so it may be good to bring in someone that you can trust and have a spiritual conversation think tank.

# Emotional Workout

You may be experiencing a plethora of emotions, or you may feel nothing at all. Whatever the case, we are about to do what we call "an emotional dump." It relieves both emotional constipation and numbness.

I want you to think about some person or incident that you are dealing with right now that provokes you in a negative way emotionally. Some of the negative emotions include anger, fear, offense, bitterness, strife, etc. Imagine that you are speaking to that person.

Unleash every thought and complaint against that person with as much verbal venom as possible. Continue to "dump" until you are either exhausted or have emotionally exploded. Allow yourself to wail before the Lord so that you can release this situation in order to gain emotional power and control.

Wailing before the Lord is cleansing and powerful.

Consider now! Send for the wailing women, send for the most skillful.

– Jeremiah 9:17

We are not called to weep silently, but to wail openly that heaven might hear us and send a solution from Zion that will fix our situation and move us forward.

It is my prayer that you wail before the Lord and use your inner trumpet and shake yourself loose.

Cry out loudly, don't hold back, raise your voice like a trumpet.

– Isaiah 58:1

Free yourself from the chains around your neck o captive daughter of Zion.

– Isaiah 52:2

We must become wailing women again, and teach our daughters to do the same...Dare to be free!

_____
_____
_____
_____
_____
_____
_____
_____
_____
_____
_____
_____
_____
_____

*Write Your World*

There's power in a pack...
Bring your sister friends
on this journey with you!

# Call to Action

Congratulations, sis! You've completed this phase of your journey to self. Give yourself a round of applause. LITERALLY go and stand in front of the mirror and clap for yourself like you are your biggest fan. We should recognize and celebrate the small wins and big victories in our lives. It is a huge step forward for you to have made this commitment to discovering and recovering yourself.

I invite you to revisit these pages to become more aware of how your thoughts, wants, and needs may change over time. Personal growth and development is meant to be a lifestyle...an on-going process. The more you learn, the more you know...the more you know, the more you grow. Anything not growing—is dead.

Get an accountability partner to help you stay on top of the hopes, goals and dreams that you have uncovered using this book. Take the time to reconnect with your renewed confidence and worthiness on a regular basis. In fact, refer the book to your friends and start an Identity in Action group; such that each of you are fully committed to showing up in life as your fully authentic self...no more fake I.D.'s!

Thank you for allowing The Color of Inspiration to help you heal through art, drama and self-discovery! It has been our pleasure to serve you.


Spiritually and Artistically Yours,

*Nevaina*

Creative Director of RAW Empowerment Productions

To contact us with feedback, testimonies or just to connect:

Email: IamNevaina@gmail.com IG/Twitter @IamNevaina Facebook.com/Nevaina

Journal your thoughts, ideas, dreams, and feelings here.

_____
_____
_____
_____
_____
_____
_____
_____
_____
_____
_____
_____
_____
_____
_____
_____
_____
_____
_____
_____
_____
_____
_____
_____
_____

*Write Your World*

# Color Theory

## *What does color say about you?*

Color theory suggests that certain colors can actually affect physical states of being. For example, look at the color red—red has been known to increase the heart rate. Conversely, the color green has been found to have a calming effect and lower heart rates. Colors also have symbolism and cultural significance. For example wearing white at a Western wedding culturally symbolizes that the bride is a virgin, but in some Eastern cultures white is the color of mourning.

Colors can evoke a mood. We are drawn to certain colors for different reasons. That reason is emotional—how it makes us feel. Or the reason maybe physical—how it makes us look. A woman's relationship to color is often intimate and intentional. It plays a part in the clothes we wear, our make-up palette, the color we dye our hair, and more.

Nature is much the same in that different flowers are clad in different colors and the sky's gradation of blues and grays depends on the "mood" set by the weather. We can connect with the colors in nature to bring balance to our emotional state and we can learn to manipulate our mood by using color. Our relationship with color can be a multidimensional experience.

Some of the suggestions of color theory can be helpful in creating a healthy connection to color, but it is not meant to be absolute. Just because the color chart says that you should like purple and you happen to really like blue…to thine own self be true. But some of the research is fascinating and can be useful.

## IS YOUR FAVORITE COLOR RED?

The language of Red, and what it communicates can be both positive and negative aspects.

Some good connotations include:

1. "Red letter day" is an expression to mark an important or significant occasion.

2. "Red carpet treatment" means to make someone feel special, or treat them like a celebrity.

3. "Paint the town red" is to celebrate, go out partying.

Bad connotations include:

1. "Seeing red" which means to be angry.

2. "In the red" describes when you are overdrawn at the bank or losing money.

3. "Red flag" denotes danger, warning, or an impending battle.

The nature of Red is that of love and war…from passionate love to violence and warfare. Red is Cupid and the Devil. Red is a hot, strong color that conjures up a range of sometimes conflicting emotions.

Studies show that red can have the physical effect of increasing the rate of respiration and raising blood pressure. The expression "seeing red" indicates anger and may stem not only from the stimulus of the color but from the natural flush (redness) of the cheeks, a physical reaction to anger, increased blood pressure, or physical exertion.

The culture of Red can be as varied as its shades, but it is nonetheless a color of presence and strength. Red represents power, hence the red power tie for business people and the red carpet for celebrities. Flashing red lights denote danger or emergency. Stop signs and stop lights are red to get drivers' attention and alert them to the dangers of the intersection.

In some cultures, red denotes purity, joy, and celebration. Red is the color of happiness and prosperity in China and may be used to attract good luck. Red is the color of mourning in South Africa; yet, it is often worn by Eastern brides. You can use the color red to grab attention and to get people to take action. When you do not want to fade into the background, red can help you stand out! Remember, a little red goes a long way.

Shades of red include: Scarlet, crimson, vermillion, carmine, maroon, burgundy, ruby, rose, madder, rouge, brick, blood red, blush, fire engine red, cinnabar, russet, rust, Venetian red, flame, Indian red, tomato.

# IS YOUR FAVORITE COLOR BLUE?

The language of blue includes feeling blue or getting the blues which represents a sadness or depression, lack of strong (violent) emotion. Blue conveys importance and confidence without being somber or sinister, hence the blue power suit of the corporate world and the blue uniforms of police officers. Long considered a corporate color, blue, especially darker blue, is associated with intelligence, stability, unity, and conservatism.

**Nature of Blue:**

As the natural color of the sky, blue is universal and studies suggests that most people like some shade of blue. The cool, calming effect of blue makes time pass more quickly and it can help you sleep so it is a good color for bedrooms. However, too much blue can dampen spirits…hence the saying "got the blues."

**Culture of Blue:**

In many diverse cultures, blue is significant in religious beliefs, brings peace, or is believed to keep the bad spirits away. In Iran, blue is the color of mourning while in the West, the "something blue" bridal tradition represents love.

**Shades of blue include:**

Indigo, turquoise, baby blue, navy, royal blue, cobalt, cerulean, Carolina blue, azure, cyan, denim, Tiffany blue, Egyptian blue, teal, periwinkle, Persian blue, powder blue, sapphire.

# IS YOUR FAVORITE COLOR GREEN?

The language of Green is that of Life and Renewal: It signifies growth, renewal, health, and environment; conversely, it has also been known to communicate envy or jealousy (green-eyed monster) or illness (puke green).

### Nature of Green:

Green is the natural color of foliage and trees and is abundant in nature. It is a restful color with some of the same calming attributes of blue. Like blue, time moves faster in a green room.

### Culture of Green:

Green is the national color of Ireland and is strongly associated with that country. Green also has close associations with Islam as it is said to be one of the colors of heaven, and the flag of the prophet Muhammad was a plain green field. In the red, black and green of the African flag, the green is said to represent the land, the black represents the people, and the red represents the blood of the people that has been shed.

### Shades of green include:

Lime, olive, viridian, jade, asparagus, mint, army green, forest green, hunter green, celadon, chartreuse, sea green, moss green, Kelly green, myrtle, emerald.

# IS YOUR FAVORITE COLOR YELLOW?

The language of yellow is that of hope and happiness as in the sunshine. When used in emergency vehicles, yellow means that hope and help are coming. It's connotative messages can be conflicting as yellow is also used to describe cowardice (yellow bellied), or sickness as in jaundice.

### The Nature of Yellow:

Commonly linked with the sun. Yellow is one of the warm colors. Because of the high visibility of bright yellow, it is often used for hazard signs and some emergency vehicles. Yellow is cheerful.

### Culture of Yellow:

For years yellow ribbons were worn as a sign of hope as women waited for their men to come marching home from war. Today, they are still used to welcome home loved ones. Its use for hazard signs creates an association between yellow and danger, although not quite as dangerous as red.

Yellow is for mourning in Egypt and actors of the Middle Ages wore yellow to signify the dead. Yet, yellow has also represented courage (Japan), merchants (India). Yellow can be a perky pick me up that is not over stimulating. Looking at a sunflower might just put a smile on your face using this theory.

### Shades of yellow include:

Gold, mustard, lemon, amber, blond, citrine, aureolin, icterine, jonquil, goldenrod, saffron, maize, urobilin, metallic gold, sunshine yellow, daisy yellow

# IS YOUR FAVORITE COLOR ORANGE?

The language of orange can be flamboyant and energetic. Its vibrancy comes from a combination of red and yellow; therefore, it shares some common attributes with these two colors. But orange has a bit less intensity or aggression than red, calmed by the cheerfulness of yellow.

### Nature of Orange:

Orange can be found in nature in the changing leaves of fall, the setting sun, and the skin and meat of citrus fruit. It is a less aggressive stimulant than red having effects on the emotions and appetite, and perhaps subliminal images of good health as it is linked to vitamin C.

### Culture of Orange:

Orange brings up images of autumn leaves, and is a color that signifies that the seasons are changing and is a color on the edge of summer and fall. When orange is combined with black it conjures images of Halloween…pumpkins and all. When used deliberately it can suggest a quiet confidence as well.

**Shades of Orange Include:**

Apricot, tangerine, salmon, terra cotta, tenne, coral, burnt orange, gamboge, peach, tangelo, pumpkin, rust, persimmon, bittersweet

# IS YOUR FAVORITE COLOR PURPLE?

The language of Purple communicates royalty and spirituality. It is seen as a mysterious color; purple is associated with both mystical things and nobility. The opposites of hot red and cool blue combine to create this intriguing color. By combining the stable and calming aspects of blue with the mystical and spiritual qualities of red, purple creates reassurance in a complex world, while adding a hint of mystery and excitement. Its opulence suggests that the kingdom is wealthy and all is well so there is no need to worry.

### Nature of Purple:

Purple has a special, almost sacred place in nature: lavender, orchid, lilac, and violet flowers are often delicate and considered precious. I imagine it being the color of the grapes that Biblical figures Joshua and Caleb saw when they spied on the promised land, which symbolized provision and prosperity. A purple room can boost a child's imagination or an artist's creativity; perhaps part of the theory around the popular children's TV character "Barney." Too much purple, like blue, could result in moodiness.

### Culture of Purple:

It is the color of mourning for widows in Thailand. Purple was said to be Cleopatra's favorite color. Purple robes are worn by royalty, people of authority, and those in high rank. It is traditionally associated with royalty in many cultures. The "Purple Heart" is a U.S. Military decoration given to soldiers bravely wounded in battle.

### Shades of Purple include:

Grape, orchid, violet, eggplant, plum, amethyst, aubergine, lilac, lavender, wisteria, royal, magenta, mauve, thistle, tyrian, pebanje.

# IS YOUR FAVORITE COLOR BROWN?

The language of brown is Earthy and deep rooted. It conveys a feeling of warmth, honesty, and wholesomeness. Although found in nature year-round, brown is often considered a fall and winter color. It is more casual than black.

### Nature of Brown:

The nature of brown is a naturally warm neutral that is found in earth, wood, and stone. It is found extensively in nature in both living and nonliving materials.

### Culture of Brown:

Brown represents wholesomeness and earthiness. While it might be considered a little on the dull side, it also represents steadfastness, simplicity, friendliness, dependability, and health. In India, brown is used as a color of mourning. Although blue is the typical corporate color, UPS (United Parcel Service) has built their business around the dependability associated with brown.

### Shades of brown include:

Cork, mahogany, dune, tan, ecru, beige, nutmeg, mocha, caramel, ochre, peanut, rum, chocolate, caramel, sienna, camel, chamois, clay, cocoa, copper, wheat, hemp, sienna, cello, umber, walnut, burgundy, coffee, bronze, honey, falu, rosewood, saddle, sandstone, tamarind, cinnamon, bile, Bordeaux, linen, melanin, Lascaux, almond, ash and the list goes on and on…

Brown has so many hues…it is beautiful and diverse just like YOU!

Couvade
Rhodes

Write your wise words here.

_____

_____

_____

_____

_____

_____

_____

Write Your World

# DAILY QUOTES

*Wise words for your soul....*

## FROM SELF, FAMILY, and OTHER FOLK...

1. Motivation will make you want to leave the bottom of the mountain, but it is the inspiration about what is at the mountain top that will give you the gas you need to make the climb.

2. Every time you open your mouth, you ought to be a motivational speaker.

3. Every day you wake up is a good day. Think you having a bad day, miss one.

4. Too weak to fight, too strong to hold on...let go and let God.

5. If you can't change the people around you...change the people around you.

6. It ain't no fun when the rabbit got the gun.

7. If you don't know where to start, start where you are.

8. The residue of your influence ought to linger with the scent of integrity, discipline and success.

9. Organized People + Organized Money = POWER.

10. If you think you will succeed or if you think you will fail, either way you are right.

11. Don't love me to death...Love Me 2 Life!

12. On their best day, no one can beat you being you.

13. Do your best and let God do the rest.

14. Favor ain't fair, but it's fun.

15. Let the world have luck; we have favor by Living Under Christ Knowledge.

16. LIFE…Living in Favor Everyday.

17. I never met a dog I had to let bark…be who You are!

18. Be great without apology.

19. Who are we to be anything less than great.

20. What one woman can do, another woman can do.

21. FEAR: False Evidence that Appears Real which leads to Frequent Excuses And Regrets.

22. The truth will make you lie.

23. The only one trapped by your inability to forgive is you.

24. When someone shows you who they are, believe them the first time.

25. Do me once shame on you; do me twice, shame on me.

26. Three sides to every story…his, hers, and the truth.

27. There is a partial truth, a whole truth, and an official truth, but only God's truth will make you free.

28. Whatever you LET is what you'll GET.

29. A hard head, makes a soft behind.

30. Inspiration moves differently than desperation.

31. You are creating your tomorrow today!

# ABOUT THE AUTHOR

## Nevaina Rhodes

Nevaina is anointed and appointed to be a Woman on a Mission and to inspire others to be the same. As unique and gifted as her name, Nevaina (Nih-von-yah) has empowered thousands of women and youth nationally and internationally.  With more than 15 years of experience as a drama therapy specialist, she has worked with divorced and transitioning professionals, adjudicated and at-risk youth, abuse survivors, doctors, lawyers, teachers and more.

She served as a Communications Specialist with the  Emory School of Law Training Program, and has been featured in many national ad campaigns, television shows and movies. It was her role as the award-winning lady in Green in the stage play "For Colored Girls…" directed by Jasmine Guy that inspired her to write The Color of Inspiration.  Nevaina is a two-time published author having also penned the soul-stirring  memoir "Conversations with Colored Girls" in which she tells of her play experience with Jasmine, Nicole Ari Parker and Robin Givens.

With a degree in broadcast journalism from the University of North Carolina at Chapel Hill, Nevaina has magnetic eloquence and charisma. She is called to be a STAR…Speak Teach Act Reach through the art of drama and the power of words. She creatively captivates women who have given themselves away, lost themselves in life, or need to re-create or rediscover themselves to find their voice, purpose and identity.

Nevaina's motto: "For the Lord is my strength and the keeper of my craft, as I share my gift with you, I pray you, too, are blessed.

Made in the USA
Monee, IL
04 January 2022